The dance must follow

The dance must follow
Sixteen cantos and an epilogue

Phil Holland

with photographs by

Moses Pendleton

Published in the United States by West Mountain Press,
an imprint of Phil Holland Voice and Word, Inc.
72 Grouse Lane, Shaftsbury, VT 05262

Print ISBN 13: 978-0-9908679-0-6
Print ISBN 10: 0990867900
E-book ISBN: 978-0-9908679-1-3
Audiobook ISBN: 978-0-9908679-2-0

Designed by Leslie Noyes, Leslie Noyes Creative Consulting, Bennington, Vermont
Printed in China by Four Colour Printing Group

Library of Congress Control Number: 2014922080
First Edition, 2015

The dance must follow from the flower

—Abū Ḥamīd bin Abū Bakr Ibrāhīm (Attar of Nishapur)

Foreword

THIS VOLUME BEGAN with an attempt by Moses Pendleton to supply a personal statement for the program of an arts benefit in Washington, Connecticut, in April, 1983. He chose to write a poem, and sketched a draft on a yellow tablet with the title "The Dancer's Craft." Some lines rhymed, some had rhythm, some consisted only of images or phrases. The irregularly lineated page resembled a plume of smoke. Moses referred to himself in the third person as "the dancer." The poem described his morning routine, which did not involve dance, as such.

The deadline was imminent. I was visiting. Moses asked my help in producing a more finished version of his lines. His original draft is either lost or lying in one of the hundreds of boxes of papers that fill the closets of his house. The first canto printed here contains some lines just as Moses wrote them and others that have been to some extent completed, altered or grafted onto his stock. In any case, it was out of this poem that the others grew. Subsequent cantos (Moses' word, recalling Byron and Shade) were also the result of a kind of collaboration, as many of them were inspired by my friend's periodic accounts of his life over the telephone. I turned his stories into verse, at a safe distance.

A few of the photographs are my own, or, in the case of the professional Momix performance photos, by Max Pucciarello, who kindly consented to their use. Most of the rest are by Moses, the dancer-photographer of Canto XV.

Phil Holland

I. The Dancer's Craft

It is the dancer's craft to choose
His mortal body as his muse,
And on the altar of his form
To lay to rest the earthly norm
Of gravity, for he must be
As light as on a lunar sea,
A living sculpture free as air,
With floating limbs and floating hair.

He rises with the feathered dawn
To put his cappuccino on –
Before the sun itself is up,
The milk is frothing in his cup –
He lights the woodstove and it throws
Heat quickly as it cranks and glows –
He cooks himself a simple bowl
Of oatmeal for his heart and soul,
Then listens to the radio's rapping,
Videotapes his fingers tapping,
Dives down into life's details,
Observes his dirty fingernails,
Finds rhythms in the room's wainscoting,
While major motion pictures plotting.

The solar rim its level ray
Darts through the woods and scatters day –
The dancer steps onto the porch
To light his body like a torch –
The sun, his overflowing health,
Are nature's easy way to wealth –
He skates and swims so he may sit
Upon his woodpile and feel fit –
He takes deep draughts of April air,
Leans back in his reclining chair
Of firewood, and falls asleep.

A cardinal sings. The minutes creep.
The porch phone rings. A voice from France
Invites the dancer to the dance.
The sun is warm, *"Pas aujourd'hui –"*
He feels such self-sufficiency
He writes no information down –
How can he think of leaving town
On such a day as this? Instead,

Let camera crews come to his bed –
It happened that way once before,
Stay put, the world will find your door,
Just keep your body bathed in light,
Your eyelids closed in second sight –

It is the dancer's craft to dream,
To let imagination teem –
Reality will follow after,
If bright and confident the crafter.

1983

II. The Fire Canto

The dancer strikes a single match –
A few dry grasses scarcely catch.
A little cone of orange light
Crackles softly into sight.
A thin smoke rises as the flames
Inch outward to extend their claims.
From blade to blade combustion creeps –
The dancer's sense of danger sleeps.

With 'major motions' on his mind,
He doesn't even feel the heat,
Till suddenly he's shocked to find
A prairie fire at his feet.

The wind picks up, and now a patch
Of thicker grass ignites like thatch.
The dancer runs to fetch a rake,
As if the fire were a snake
That he might beat to death – instead,
He fans the flames a fiercer red,
The tool itself becomes a torch,

His pants begin to smoke and scorch,
He stamps and leaps, as if to dance,
His sneakers melt, the flames advance.

A ring of fire spreads so wide
That sunflowers burn on every side.
Like an exploding star, the fire
Flares ever outward, the entire
Field is burning, soon the woods,
Nor far his neighbor's house and goods.

The call goes out for volunteers –
In minutes a brigade appears.
The Fire Marshall gives a shout –
In minutes the inferno's out.

The dancer's fined, the hoses reeled –
Smoke drifts above the blackened field.

1986

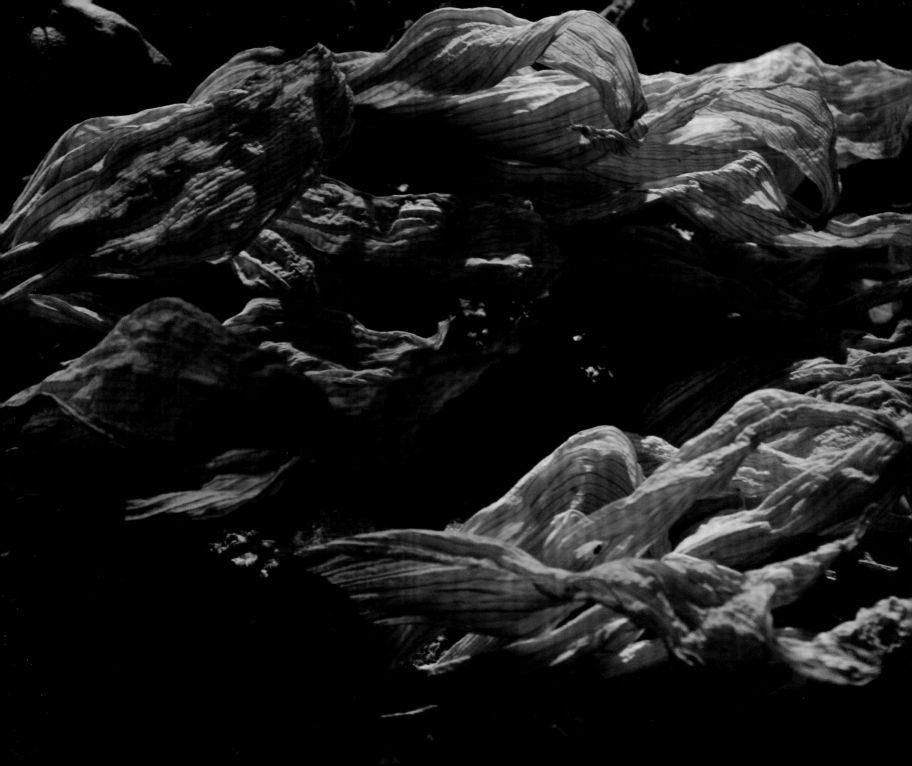

III. The Pimm's Canto

One day, on the word of Moses
Pendleton, whose nose is
Very good in such whims,
I bought a bottle of Pimm's.

I took a nip,
No more than wet my lip –
There must have been a ship
In the bottle.

I seemed to sail a sea of shining topaz –
I must have stopped at islands where the spices
Inebriate the organs of perception.
There was an herb half bitter,
There was a fruit whose peel –
There was root whose power
Is to heal –
There was a tender flower
That made the heavens reel.

This Pimm's is light and fiery,
I thought, and can inspire me.

We who are poets languish
Unless we're lifted up
In spirit by a nectar
Like a No. 1 Pimm's Cup.

A cheering morning cordial,
A pickup each afternoon,
A comfort in the evening,
Companion by the moon.

And I thought of my friend in his castle –
In his house with the turret of brass –
Sitting there by a window whose pane is
Convex like the rim of a glass.

When the afternoon turns amber,
And you raise the antique shades
Of your chamber in the tower,
As the daylight slowly fades,
And you sip your Pimm's to music,
And it gleams with tints of red,
And the harp strings wink and shimmer,
Swim and glimmer in your head,

Then films arise before your eyes
And then you seem to see
Yourself in motion pictures
Given immortality.

Night comes, the guests are knocking,
The ball begins below –
A hundred tongues are talking
In the fire's social glow –
And each hand holds a crystal cup,
And each hand tends a flame –
See how the people drink it up,
Hear as they sound the name
Of Pimm's.

Candles in candelabras
Flicker madly in the halls –
Photographic metamorphoses
Peer down from peeling walls –

The house becomes a temple,
And now the rites proceed –
Pimm's is the libation,
The idol, and the creed.

Goblets, mirrors, chandeliers
Dance with reflected light –
The guests have rolled away the rugs
And dance away the night.

The dawning finds you on the porch,
Enjoying a glass of Pimm's –
How it revives the senses,
How it restores the limbs.

A substitute for coffee,
A replacement for toast and jam,
As nourishing as yogurt,
Sustaining as eggs and ham.

A healthy, herbal breakfast,
A creative working lunch,
A self-sufficient banquet,
And universal punch.

Dr. Holland has prescribed it
In everlasting ink,
And now he leaves off rhyming
To pour himself another little drink
Of Pimm's.

1987

IV. Rebecca

All Hallows' Eve – the moon is full,
A bonfire burns between
The lunar garden's faded horns,
And it makes a pretty scene.

A ten-foot hedge encloses
On three sides the lawn and porch –
In this outdoor theater Moses
Nightly burns a pitch-pine torch.

But tonight the pine's augmented
With whole limbs of ash and oak
That he's gathered from his forests,
Where they fell without a stroke.

To this rite of fall come dancers –
Where they step is their studio –

A woman with a sunflower staff,
Two elk-like men with sticks,
And a cameraman in a checkered robe
Who is master of the mix.

The men vault through the fire
To the beating of a drum,
So they might feel for a moment
Just a lick of martyrdom.

To the snapping of the fagots
And the twisting of the sparks,
The initiate advances
With a smile like Joan of Arc's.

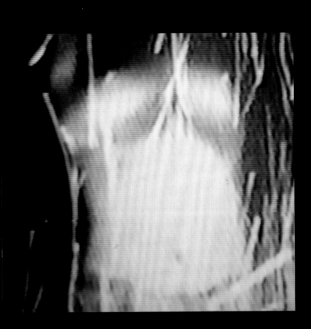

The fire bakes and singes,
Waves of white heat arise –
Rebecca stands up steadfast
Till the scorching sweatshirt flies.

The firelight like footlights
Strikes her nostrils and her neck,
As in some paintings by Degas,
Or else Toulouse-Lautrec.

Or the light that Loie Fuller
In her famous Fire Dance
Shone on her whirling body
As she slipped into a trance.

The isolating camera
Towards its subject slowly twirls –
The long athletic torso,
The wide mouth full of pearls.

Her Polynesian shoulders
And breasts that seem to rise –
She looks into the camera
With Frida Kahlo eyes.

Her face is almost African –
The flames that shoot beneath
Shadow her eyes while dazzling
Her throat, her chin, her teeth.

Like Liberty she raises
One arm upward to the sky,
She seems to float above the clouds
Of sparks that burst and fly.

Rebecca in slow motion lifts
Her eyes up high, and higher,
To face the moon, while stretching
Her bright body to the fire.

V. The Midlife Canto

He returns from old Milano
To take up whatever's new,
And finds the next day Anno
Domini he's 42.

Picasso, San Francisco,
Faxes to be unfurled,
A feature film in Arizona,
Crates of Momix for the world.

On the sun-drenched porch below which
Melting ice has made a moat,
He perches on his woodpile
As if it were a swinging oat.

Cappuccino, marijuana,
Dripping snowmelt mixed with Pimm's,
And the morning sun a sauna
Spreading heart's ease through his limbs.

The dancer sniffs the ginger air,
Imagination spins,
The West Wind wakes the old March hare,
Another year begins.

March 1991

VI. The Long Hot Summer

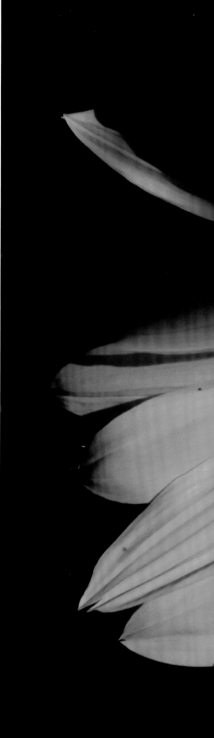

The day star, angry at the moon's eclipse,
A track of fire lays across the land –
The wilting earth looks up with parching lips,
As fertile soil is turned to desert sand.

In Moses' field the great design
Of living plants is in decline –
The sunflowers, too thickly sown,
By mid-July are scarce half grown,
With spindly stalks and leaves too small,
That should be strong and broad and tall.
Their crowded roots contract in pain,
Just holding on to hopes of rain.
Alone in all the flaming sky
The sun looks down with lidless eye.

Moses beholds the set-to-be
In horror that the CBC
Will find it withered, stunted, brown,
Which was their cause of coming down.
Alas, too easily untracked,
He anguishes, but cannot act.

He makes a call and summons forth
A fellow gardener from the north –
The friend who first had laid the rays
Returns and solemnly surveys.
No sooner is inspection made
Than there is talk of a brigade.
But first the brigadiers extend
Four garden hoses end to end
Across the lawn and through the hedge
Right to the garden's upper edge.
The waters flow, but quickly sink,
So dying is the earth for drink.
The project fails, but will endures –
One watered plant the rest secures.

The day's events are told at table,
Where Cynthia, the ever able
Cynthia, conceives a plan –
A swimming pool fill-upper man
Must come to flood the flower field.
The Yellow Pages quickly yield
A name – "Pete's Pools – Construction, Filling" –
And number – called – and Pete is willing.

The urgent summons telephonic
Is answered from the Housatonic –
A truck with 7,000 gallons
Arrives to re-set nature's balance.
Three burly men burst from the cab,
Adjust their red suspenders, grab
The hoses, haul, and swear and shout
To "let the friggin' river out!"
Right underneath the midday sun
The shining waters gush and run –
Two hours of heatstroke sun are braved,
The sunflowers are soaked, and saved.

To Rome to beat the Momix drums
Goes Moses, and a heatwave comes.
The sun his raving horses beats,
New England suffers jungle heats.
But the more the temperature exceeds,
The more the flowers grow like weeds,
Regain their strength, shoot up their suns,
And summer into August runs.

As CBC men board their train
In Montreal, a hurricane
Named Bob decides to have his way
Until he's leveled every ray.
The drowned and beaten flowers lie
Like battle dead beneath the sky.

The crew arrives, contacts its leaders,
And quickly rents a row of cedars.
A hedge is dug in for the day,
The shooting done, it's trucked away –
The movie will be shown in May.

1991

VII. The Carbon Self

He's temporarily disabled,
Which brings on a fear of death,
So he takes a tip from Whitman
And he worships his own breath.

He collects his conversations,
Mile on mile of running tape,
Lest the gas of his creations
Should escape.

He is free to leave his senses
If the tape recorders roll,
And his fax machine dispenses
Tape transcriptions by the scroll.

Every day arts correspondents
Ask him all about his muse –
The truth is that she used to dance,
But now gives interviews.

And when they ask what Momix is,
"What isn't it?" he replies,
But if they try a second time,
He specifies:

"Momix is an elixir,
It's a precious drug, a potion,
It's a tonic, it's a mixer,
Imagination given motion.

"It's a water cure, a fountain
Of youth, a lake, a pool,
It's a castle on a mountain,
It's a garden, it's a school.

"It's a vision in the fire,
It's a vein of fantasy,
Feeding physical desire,
Flooding light and energy.

"It is holy human freedom,
And divine creative will,
It's the devil when you need him,
It's our life on this green hill – "

Then he tells about the moment,
And proclaims the carbon self
(Meanwhile thinking that his words
Exist to end up on a shelf).

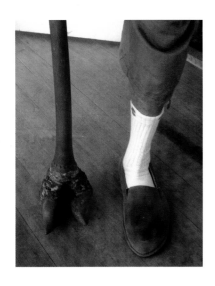

He says the spirit is a wick,
And that the body's fuel
To burn until the final flick-
Er's utmost molecule.

He says the craft of dancing
Is to burn with a gem-like flame,
An audience for oxygen,
And critics for a name.

🖋

He is all anticipation
For some filming by a Scot,
And the exquisite sensation
Every day of being shot.

The crew will come to get a feed
At his Litchfield County cottage,
In answer to his inner need
To turn life into footage.

He will give a little tour
Of his closets and his halls,
Where the wallpaper like parchment
Peels in pages from the walls,

And his rooms and writing tables,
With their crystals and their pens,
Screenplays and yellow tablets,
Reviews, and candle-ends.

The subject of the special
Is the making of a show –
"Behind the scenes with Moses"
And his singular m.o. –

The camera will record it all –
But this time it never arrives –
The project's killed – it vanishes –
The written word survives.

1993

24

VIII. The Clementine Canto

On a singing summer morning,
At his table on the porch,
Moses looks out on his gardens,
Where a sunflower, like a torch,

Catches full in its corona
The first rays of golden sun –
Its companions, by the hundreds,
Follow after, every one.

Facing eastward, all the flowers
Drink the sunlight at its source,
Then reflect it back on Moses
As the day's creative force.

Close to hand a cappuccino,
And a slice of whole wheat bread,
The official Red Sox Yearbook,
There is "Baseball" in his head.

Bumblebees like grazing bison
Roam each blooming solar disk,
Deep in sweet and yellow prairies,
You disturb them at your risk.

Drunk with nectar, dripping pollen,
Gold dust loaded on their thighs,
They have found their El Dorado
And the fields of Paradise.

With his macroscopic camera
Aimed directly at a bee,
Moses moves in for a close-up,
Till the insect angrily

Stings the surface of the macro-
Scopic lens as if to kill,
But instead of death produces
An intense aesthetic thrill.

For the lens is like the porthole
Of a Beebe bathyscaphe,
It was by such explorations
Moses learned to choreograph.

Mammoth Russian, Giant Grey Stripe,
Multi-headed Henry Wilde,
Sole d'Oro, Autumn Beauty,
Music Box Mix for a child.

Wreathed in sepals, coiled in spirals,
Seeds begin to energize,
Tender petals blinking open,
Timelapse flare of yellow eyes.

Popping flashbulbs, signal beacons,
Lanterns strung along a line,
Sunny faces, floral people,
Ten feet tall and feeling fine.

Solar glory, all too fleeting,
As the summer hours fly,
Heavy seedheads bending earthward,
Twisting slowly as they dry.

Preparation for the banquet
Takes up all the afternoon,
For the dancers, it's rehearsal,
Forty guests are coming soon.

Momix women, summer dresses,
Yellow flowers in their hair,
Pollen falling on their shoulders,
Greet arrivals by the stair.

To the porch for conversation,
Sunflower nuts, and fine champagne,
Moses dressed in his cream colors,
Looking rather like Mark Twain.

To the tower for the sunset
And a view of earth below,
Sixteen rays around a circle,
You can see the garden glow.

As the dusk falls, Tiki torches
Guide the guests to follow on
Through an alley made of flowers
To the circle made of lawn.

In the center of the circle
Of the radiating rays,
Citronella smokes like incense,
Beeswax candles calmly blaze.

Thirteen tables laid with dinner
Are arranged to make a cross,
Ripe tomatoes and fresh pasta,
Homemade pesto for the sauce.

Moses wears a smoking jacket
With a pin of amethyst,
Round his head a poet's garland,
Round his feet the evening mist.

As the dew falls and the guests drink,
And the host drinks, laughs, and reels,
In his constant tape recorder
Condensation slows the wheels.

As the torches burn to sockets,
There arises in the East,
Like a ghostly orange wafer,
The full Corn Moon on the feast.

Then it's indoors for some dancing,
Coffee, cake, and firelight,
Till the dawn breaks and the day ends,
And the moon slips out of sight.

1994

IX. The Lost Canto

For twenty years the living rays
Have brightened Moses' summer days –
Or else, when some mischance befell,
Have lit his way to living hell.

Around a clover circle
Sixteen fingers single file
Array their giant flowers
Like a dial.

Two-acre time-teller,
Spiral-seeded field-filler,
Yellow-petalled eye-opener,
Heart-leaved *Helianthus,*
Twenty circling years.

Many tillers since the time that one,
Remembering a Zuni sun,
Carved in the earth with churning tines
Rows for plants like Nazca lines.

Many have tended the garden
Since, and stood for photographs,

Girls with tanned shoulders dusted with pollen,
Men like centurions holding their staffs,
And Moses drunken lord of summer
With camera in his hand and crown of flowers,
Or working like the meanest peasant
To make the scene for others pleasant.

Twenty years of war against woodchucks,
Meadow-mice, chipmunks, and moles,
With poisons, traps, and ultrasound,
And smoke-bombs in their holes –
Searing drought and spreading fire,
Thunderstorm and hurricane,
Careless gardeners for hire,
Crows and weeds and acid rain.

This summer, further setbacks –
A wet spring breeding soil-borne diseases,
Verticillium wilt stalking the field like the plague,
Black spots climbing the stems and withering leaves –
Then Moses away in July, a Berliner,
While the populous deer of Judea
Came and cropped every flower for dinner.

The dancer returned to a field of death,
Scarcely a leaf was left, disaster.
Staggering down the blasted rays in shock,
Beating the ground and shaking his fists
At the woman named Laura, who was to watch over,
He collapsed in despair in the clover.

When he rose, it was for battle –
Immediate application of Milorganite
And deer-repelling Ropel.
Bellowing half-mad from his bedroom window at dawn
At the grazing deer on the lawn placid as llamas,
Roaring out of the house, bursting through the hedge
(Sudden thundering hooves), tearing his pajamas –
He did this every single day
Until the deer would stay away.

And every evening when the light
Is long and green and softly bright,
Hydrotherapeutic Moses
Healed his wounded plants with hoses,
Stirring every flower's roots
To send one final set of shoots,
Until a bud, a leaf, a stem,
Appeared in pairs on all of them.

The summer is not over.
Although there'll be no glory
Of arching mammoth blooms,
There is time before October
For shoots by the hundreds to flare into flowers
Like late-summer meteor showers.

On a cool September evening
Let the Corn Moon beam
On a resurrected garden,
Let a table be set in the circle,
And dancers appear bearing wine,
Let Laura raise a glass
To never-dying Nature,
And Moses with his shepherd's crook
(One of last year's fourteen-footers)
Lead out the deer herd from the woods,
The great stag and his does,
To feed on grain at the edge of the garden.
Let the ghost of Pudge the cat arise
To hunt again on the luminous dial –
In the perfect stillness before she springs,
Let the time show: twenty years.

1999

X. The Millennium Canto

A ball of bubbled amber
Gleams at sunset on the porch –
The dying sun is flaming like a torch –
The last red rays are streaming
Deep inside the amber ball –
The dancer in his wicker chair
Is sitting motionlessly there,
Making steam from winter air,
And dreaming on it all.

A hundred tapes inside the door
Lie scattered on the study floor –
The voices of departed years
Speak daily in the dancer's ears –
He takes them on his oakwood walk,
And on the snowy paths they talk
Of films and moons and meetings,
Of sunflowers and Momix shows
(A cork pops and the champagne flows),
And all his life's exceedings.

The dark comes on, he rises up
To chase the sun from floor to floor –
He opens up the attic door
And climbs the cold and creaky stair
Into the tower chamber, where
Ten thousand tapes lie deep,
Where in the night rats rumble,
And tapes tumble,
And below, he cannot sleep.

Higher – up the ladder to the roof
To watch the sinking sun
In the new millennium –
How rapidly it drops from sight,
While up above, the clouds alight
Cast rose and amber over all –
With lifted hands
The dancer stands
Beneath the glowing ball
Of heaven stretching high and wide –
Like a rising bubble trapped inside.

January 2000

XI. The Sunflower Canto

Late summer sunflower splendor,
Veins of bright gold in the rays,
An occasion to add to the story
Of how Moses passes his days.

Each morning in his yellow cap
He swims in Tom's blue waters,
His strokes across the lake and back
As easy as an otter's.

Then to his gardens to survey
The progress of each flower,
He sees some changes every day,
On some days, every hour.

He lingers often by a stem
With heart-shaped leaves outspread,
Smooth, rounded shoulders, girlish neck,
And nodding, golden head.

For he's a flower lover,
And he's taken a sunflower bride,
He washes her feet with Miracle-Gro,
And poses by her side.

In the circle with the sixteen rays
The dancer seeks his visions –
Across the street the company prays
For him to reach decisions.

From the center of the circle
To the corners of the world,
Momix shoots along the flight paths
And the fantasy's unfurled.

"Opus Cactus" in Verona,
"Passion" in Santa Fe,
"Baseball" in Barcelona,
"In Orbit" in Paraguay.

The show's the dream of art, a rite
Of moving bodies, music, light,
The sweet illusion of an hour,
As transitory as a flower.

On every soul who comes to see
It scatters golden energy,
Inviting all, before it's done,
To walk with Moses in the sun.

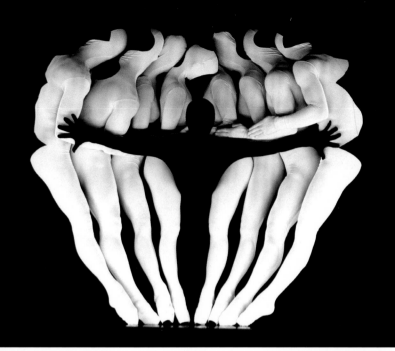

In Sydney or in Budapest
The show begins – meanwhile,
In Tom's blue waters Moses swims
Another dreamy mile.

The time has come for sacrifice,
He walks the colonnade,
Like an Aztec with obsidian,
And he wields a silver blade.

In bottles when the wine is drunk,
In vases cut like crystals,
The severed heads are firmly sunk,
With pollen-dusted pistils.

His table like an altar
Is decked with votive flowers,
He holds communion with the press
On the telephone for hours,

And dwells in his summer palace,
A man (when not at work) at ease,
The master of his plantation,
And lord of the bumblebees.

The alchemists maintain the world
Will turn to gold someday,
And that their mystic processes
Just speed things on their way.
That is, if you increase the rate
A hundred or a thousandfold
At which the elements advance,
You'll cook yourself a pot of gold.

This every gardener well knows,
Who in a single season grows
Fields of gold by tilling, seeding,
Fertilizing, watering, weeding,
Repelling deer, suppressing moles,
And bombing woodchucks in their holes –
So by these arts both fine and bold
Transforming every green to gold.

Gold, gold, golden flowers,
From seeds in earth in summer hours
They sprout and shoot and burst and bloom
Till gold fills every room.

Gold on the tables,
Gold on the chairs,
Heaped in the corners,
Hung from the stairs.

Gold coronas everywhere,
Halos of gold like Eastern saints,
Beautiful girls with golden hair,
The gold of Vincent's Provence paints.

On every surface pollen
In golden circles fallen,
The air itself with golden grains
Glitters in twisting sunbeam chains.

What better way to pass the hours
Than with these golden flowers?

Sunflower sunflower
Second to none flower
Spirally spun flower
Each year begun flower
Wonderful fun flower
Able to stun flower
Many in one flower
Follow-the-sun flower
Follow the sunflower.

2000

XII. Summer of 2002

The spinning earth goes circling round
The sun, and spring returns –
A thirst for summer glory
In the dancer's bosom burns.

Sunflowers are his passion,
Their annual cycle his muse –
The daylight daily lengthens
Till there is no time to lose.

He scrutinizes catalogues
For varieties that will thrive –
The seedsmen weave their rhapsodies,
Rattling packets soon arrive.

Crumbly antique hen manure
Is worked into the fresh-plowed rays
And other plots and patches
On sunny April days.

In May, while birds are singing,
Moses presses in each seed –
He thumps the earth above them
Until his fingers bleed.

This year he's growing Cyclops,
Named for its one great eye
That swings atop a mighty stalk
Fifteen feet in the sky.

Other lesser kinds are Mammoth,
Giant Grey Stripe, and King Kong,
Double Dandy, Autumn Beauty,
Orange Sun, Strawberry Blonde.

And one marked simply "Sunflower"
With a picture of a man
On a ladder by his rooftop
With a flower in his hand.

"Our beautiful bright yellow
Giants are a joy to grow –
These towering blooms are guaranteed
To put on quite a show."

A show – and this a summer
To surpass all those before,
And cultivate a garden
While others talk of war.

The great design in his backyard
Is sensational, and yet,
The dancer's always dreaming
Of an ever grander set.

He used to grow some vegetables,
Now it's sunflowers short and tall,
Velvet Queen and Primrose Yellow,
And there are no paths at all.

Paul Bunyan in the compost,
Ring of Fire one strip wide,
A circle of Sol below the hedge,
A crescent moon inside.

At Quincy's farm a mile away
There lies another patch –
Its four rows stretch two football fields,
And the weeds are thick as thatch.

The dancer's planted every seed
And watered every flower –
He pulls the weeds at terrific speed,
While his helper pulls by the hour.

Yet still they sprout, so his dancers
Arrive like a human hoe –
Their bodies swing to music
As they lay the witchgrass low.

Now as for Mother Nature,
She's fickle, she's perverse –
She showers you with blessings,
Then tosses in a curse.

Creator of all flowers,
But also wilts and blights,
The friendly forest creatures,
And their savage appetites.

For deer will crop the tender stalks,
And squirrels will eat the seeds,
And woodchucks gnaw on all that's raw
To satisfy their needs.

But Moses has a strategy,
He attracts, and he repels –
He feeds whole herds of wildlife
While diffusing certain smells.

Almost daily he disgorges
Bags of seed at one safe site –
Then dopes his plants with Bobex,
Liquid Fence, and Milorganite.

Organic these repellents,
But the deer prefer free lunch –
Exploding populations
Of squirrels just sit and munch.

Walking slowly through his fields,
He applies Bill's Spray-N-Grow
(A fish emulsion) to each leaf,
Squirting Root Guard down below.

The water from his spring-fed well
Is always fresh and cold,
He sprays, and rainbows glisten
Above each plant of gold.

Like beanstalks (magic beanstalks)
The stems shoot toward the skies –
Visions of thousands of swinging blooms
In the dancer's head arise.

Visions of Momix girls dancing
With sunflower heads in their hair,
Their men at attention with sunflower staffs,
Yellow eyes popping high in the air.

Visions of seeds in tight spirals
Swelling through long summer days,
Exploding in autumn in ecstasy
To the cries of the plundering jays.

"Moses, the limo is leaving!
You'd better just come as you are –
The plane leaves at eight, we're going to be late,
Drop those hoses and get in the car!"

No – he's not going –
For now is the time
To sit with the blooms
At the peak of their prime.

He spends the long green afternoon
At the heart of a plot planted tight,
Flower arms reaching around him,
And above, suns that block out the light.

Alone in this sunflower jungle,
Like Yeats in his bee-loud glade,
He loses himself in his headphones,
Watching leaves oscillate in the shade.

Then come storms – and the summer is over!
The flowers are bent in the rays,
The press is demanding his presence,
And the house is in need of bouquets.

The dancer draws his silver knife
In the fields of Quincy Farm –
Paul Bunyans fall like redwoods
In the cradle of his arm.

He hauls them home, then ranges
In his field of gold and jade –
His left hand holds the straining necks,
His right hand wields the blade.

Thirty vases are positioned
In his living and dining rooms
For the dancer-flower-arranger
To feng-shui them full of blooms.

The ceilings are high, the vases,
Some of them, three feet tall –
The giant suns surround you so
You cannot see the wall.

The effect is somewhat similar
To living in a flower bowl –
That is, if you were an insect
And had perched on a petiole.

And all this display just a setting
For receiving the *New York Times* –
And for giving me – I'm not forgetting –
Another harvest season's rhymes.

September 2002

48

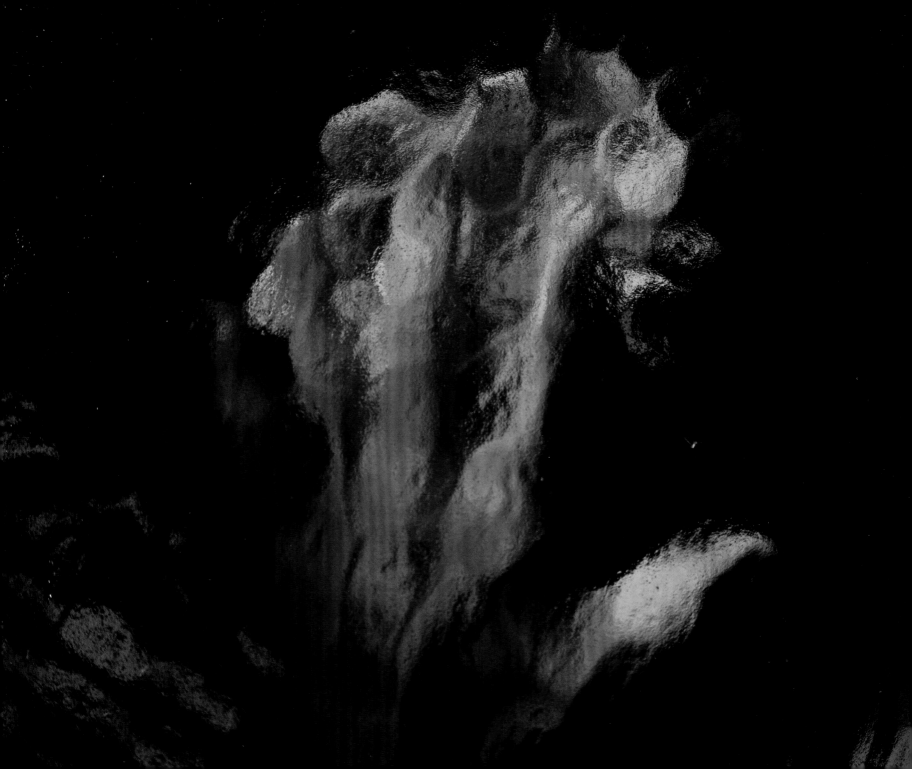

XIII. 9/11/2002

It had been 96 degrees,
The atmosphere was thick and wet
That had been sitting upon Nature,
And was sitting yet.

At last the weatherman foretold
That a mass of clear and dry
Canadian air was coming,
Though with winds that might be high.

Then no one thought of the weather –
The 11th of September
Had dawned, and all Americans
Stood ready to remember.

The ceremony in New York
Was solemn, grim, and grand,
When a passing gust of wind
Whipped up a cloud of dust and sand.

The whirlwind rose and vanished
Where once the towers were –
Meanwhile, in Litchfield County,
The leaves began to stir.

The dancer saw the evil gust
On CNN, what could it mean?
He stepped outside to ruminate
On his world of gold and green.

As he paced among his flowers,
He photographed every one,
By the hundreds standing, stooping –
Their lives too would soon be done.

The haze was lifting and a breeze
Was blowing from the north –
It cleared the air and calmed the mind
And led the dancer forth

Upon his bike to Quincy Lane,
Where the harvest would soon be ready –
He videotaped the tossing heads,
For the breeze was rather steady.

The upright full round flowers
Would be perfect for display –
The triumph of the summer
Was less than a week away.

He strokes out towards the pocket
With the perches and the pikes,
When out of the clear September sky
The windstorm strikes.

The sun is shining brightly
But the firmament has cracked –
The crystal day is shattered,
For the north wind has attacked.

Suddenly there are whitecaps,
And seas running two feet high,
With slapping waves and flying spray
That spits in the dancer's eye.

His flowers! Now he churns for shore
To bring the harvest home –
Not Byron in the Hellespont
Swam faster through the foam.

Desperately the dancer drags
His body on the beach –
His towel is snapping in the gusts
In a branch he cannot reach.

He speeds away in his black sedan,
Then brakes hard, for a tree is down
Across the road by Rumsey Hall –
He will have to drive through town.

Power lines are falling
And sparking in the streets,
An oak, uprooted, heaves to earth,
He swerves, he swears, he cheats

Death at several corners – home,
He gains the porch, and there
Sees papers, flowers, and a phone
All whirling in the air.

Out in the lunar garden
A hail of walnuts falls –
He dashes through the hedges,
And what he sees appalls.

Sunflowers are careening,
One great stem just blows apart –
The crack is like a rifle
Bullet to the heart.

But for now, the flowers were dancing
In long swaying lines on the land –
Amid remembrances of death
Here was life in bloom at hand.

Back to the house, off to the lake
To take his daily swim –
The waters stream before the wind
And sparkle up at him.

Back in the car,
Off to the Farm,
Hoping his beauties
Will not come to harm.

But the Farm is on a hilltop,
And the unresisted gale
Is threshing through the flowers
Like a flail.

Their heads are swinging madly,
Like clanging bells they crash,
Coughing seeds up in their agony
Under the northern lash.

Moses calls on Mother Nature
To stop beating her only child –
She answers tearing through the field
With the power of the Wild.

The Cyclops are raging, the Mammoths berserk,
Orange Suns like stampeding giraffes,
The vigorous Kong, so gigantically strong,
Pound gargantuan leaves on their staffs.

The dancer looks to heaven,
The sky is clear as glass –
The wind that now is blowing,
This too, he knows, shall pass.

The following day the destruction
Is colossal, and the air is chill –
The dancer's in shock, in the evening
Candles burn in the house on Bell Hill.

The suns that remain have no petals,
The ranks that are standing are thinned,
The leaves hanging down are withered and brown,
As if scorched by a nuclear wind.

But the sprouts that the season began with
Are now seeds on the face of the earth –
By the thousands they lie, fallen out of the sky,
In the soil that will give them rebirth.

And the dancer recovers, though slowly,
As he walks day by day through his fields,
Where he sees devastation producing
Forms of beauty that peace never yields.

The twisted sepals gripping
In death the massive heads,
The bent, tucked arms of flowers down
And dreaming in their beds.

The finger shapes of side-shoots
Reach up from the flattened stems –
The fields will soon be filled again
With golden diadems.

And the dancers are rehearsing
In the studio day and night –
They stretch and spring and float and swing
As if growing toward the light.

To New York, where the city's still reeling
From the storm and the deaths from the skies,
Moses soon will be going with Momix,
And the hearts of the people will rise.

September 2002

XIV. Home Alone

Coffee, quiet, afternoon,
Light crackles in the dining room –
A shadow passes on the wall
With cup in hand, the dancer's all
Alone at home this afternoon,
His head as flooded as the room.

On sideboards crystals vibrate
And sunflowers bare their breasts,
Open books disclose their secrets
In the place of dinner guests.

The moon-faced clock in the corner
Has never been heard to chime –
For twenty-three years its painted lips
Have been sealed against the time.

On the wall grandfather Moses
At the height of all his powers
Sits at his desk surrounded
By men, and flags, and flowers.

In ranks on every wainscot
Stand photographs three tiers deep,
In every drawer the faces
Of the past their features keep.

The light grows slowly sepia,
Images come in waves,
The past swirls in a maelstrom,
Every detail – Moses saves.

His house is a time treasury,
A relic-littered shrine,
He plays a tape from '83
And voices flow like wine.

It's his presidential palace,
Where he – or his double – dwells,
It's his private little paradise
And home to his private hells.

It's his personal chamber theater,
It's his live-in movie set,
The scene of his latest picture,
Only he hasn't released it yet –

The dancer bends to read a book,
The Secret Teachings of All Ages –
An alchemist returns his look –
A shadow turns the pages.

2003

XV. Another Summer

Another summer – the 25th –
But what is time compared to myth? –
Finds Moses once more with his flowers
Most of his waking hours.
The time he used to give to dance
He now devotes to raising plants –
But ask the reason he's immersing
Himself in soil, he says, "Rehearsing –
I grow my dances from the seed,
Let others choreograph, I weed –
The sun, the earth, they are the force
Behind all moving things, the source
Alike of my creative power –
The dance must follow from the flower.
I'm not the first to work this way –
Just think, for instance, of Monet,
Who, when his neighbors found it odd
To see the painter hack the sod,
Said, 'Chers amis, mais je pioche,
I use the hoe before the brush,
My gardens are a work of art,
Of which I've painted only part.'"

The Cyclops rise in solar order,
With extra plantings in the border,
And little circles in the lawn,
Like moons, to grow new kinds upon,
Lemon Aura, Hopi Black Dye,
Supermane, and Tiger Eye.

To Quincy's fields a mile away
The dancer cycles every day –
In that sweet soil he laid a row
Of sunflowers, several years ago,
To have fresh heads in quick supply
Whenever guests were coming by –
Each row a stretching line of plants as
Long as those of corn in Kansas,
Long as the earth, tall as the sky –
A hundred yards, that is, by ten feet high.
But so as not to waste a seed
This year, beyond all need
Of fresh bouquets for porch and table,
The dancer sowed all he was able –
Four rows, then eight, and then some more,
Until he'd almost sown a score.

He tamped the earth in every row
With sideways step like a Navaho.
On every spreading leaf he sprayed
A special mixture he had made
Of fish emulsion, Super Bobex,
Miracle-Gro, and a dash of Momix.

The grass, like art itself, is long –
Soon Moses senses something's wrong.
Faintness, and a general ache,
A fever burning in the lake,
Sharp chills beneath the midday sun,
No energy – all lead to one
Conclusion, as the doctor sees,
The dancer has caught Lyme Disease.
In that long grass, a tiny tick
Had sucked his blood and made him sick.

While Moses languishes in bed,
Down in the garden up pops the head
Of *Marmota monax*, who smells his chance
To feast at will on Moses' plants.
The hungry woodchuck munches
Sunflowers for his lunches,
Like a bruin in a berry patch,
And in size he grows almost a match.

He digs a den at the garden's edge,
Deep inside the hawthorn hedge
Guarded by a million bees,
And lives at his rodent's ease.

When *Homo sapiens* (call him Moses)
Revives, he howls and shakes his hoses.
Grimly pale, on hands and knees
He refills rows by slow degrees
With transplants, and he sets his traps,
While *monax* watches, waits, and naps.
On he raids at dawn undaunted,
Till Moses gives him what he wanted:
Tender young salads grown at his door,
Mesclun, radicchio, arugula, more
Sweet little sunflowers, with succulent tips –
Till these prove a distraction
And cut short his trips.

Meanwhile away at Quincy Lane
The cutting garden grows like cane.
Moses returns to long arcades
Between the rows, with dancing shades,
Green alleys where he walks for hours

Photographing flowers –
It's not alone the image that attracts,
But also the repeated instant acts
Of looking through the lens and squeezing,
Followed by that sudden freezing
Of form and color in a frame
That light has painted with its flame.

In little more than two short months,
Two thousand golden swinging suns,
A green and yellow mile of bloom,
Are ready for the dining room.
The dancers have returned from Rome,
And they will bring the harvest home.
They cut the stalks and bear the loads
Like reapers down the leafy roads
To waiting house and studio,
Until the rooms all overflow
With flowers, and the smell of plants
Intoxicates, and then the dance
Is ready to begin,
The studio to spin,
The summer show what it has been.

2005

XVI. The Sixteenth Canto

I'll try a sixteenth canto,
The last one, I suppose,
Since someone has suggested
That I match the sixteen rows,

Or rays, as I have called them,
Which these days are marigolds,
Since they don't appeal to varmints,
And resist most wilts and molds.

Don't worry, still the dancer
Cultivates *Helianthus*,
Like Monet his water lilies,
And also his *Agapanthus*.

Yet even this year the marigolds
Were blackened by the blight
That wiped out all those tomatoes
From New York to Lubec Light.

The blight – I frankly hesitate
To tell of another disaster –
Began with rain, and then more rain
Followed fast, and followed faster,

(I know, I stole that line from Poe –)
Until the water table
Had risen above the land and made
It indistinguishable.

The farmers, and the dancer,
Stood helpless as their seed
Rotted or sent a feeble stem
Up for the blight to breed.

Planting and replanting,
Moses waited for the sun,
Which didn't come till August
When the race was almost run.

Yet even then he rushed to sow
A sixty-day variety,
And gave his seedlings Miracle-Gro,
And hoed for his anxiety.

But let's rewind the tape a bit:
A man, a plan, a panic, a
New piece called
"Botanica."

One January evening
It opened at the Warner,
In Torrington, Connecticut,
Which is right around the corner.

Convenient, when it doesn't snow
All day and night a foot or so –
But people came, the show went on,
And seemed from life to have been drawn:

The stage is locked in winter,
And then the seasons swing
Around to start the North's
Annual awakening.

A trickle's soon a torrent,
And bodies made of snow
Arise out of the river's
Inexorable flow.

A flock of geese honks overhead,
Below, in clear spring pools,
Life quickens microscopically
What the spinning Earth unspools.

An alabaster swan alights,
A pond nymph spreads her wings,
Each creature preens and gazes
At its own imaginings.

The Worm Moon rising, in the soil
The worms begin to turn,
A sprout emerges from a seed,
A spore becomes a fern.

A dinosaur – its bones, at least –
Mates with a daffodil,
The very rocks rise up and walk –
Make of this what you will.

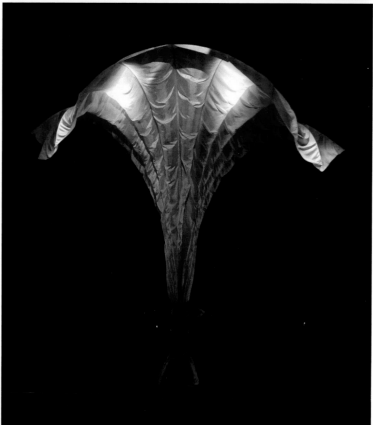

The flowers dance, like Disney
On drugs, and then the bees,
In ways that would have shocked von Frisch,
Shake their anatomies.

Above a darkling meadow,
Winking insects interweave
Their lanterns as the centaurs leap
On a mild Midsummer Eve.

A thunderstorm (recorded live)
Electrifies the hall,
A spider's web with diamonds
Strung is perfect for the ball.

Deep in the heart of summer,
The sun with shining torso
Is working in the fields all day,
Like Moses – only more so.

The oakwood twirls its golden trees,
A pale *Datura* bloom
Unfolds in many colors
Its vespertine perfume.

Or is it the first snowflake,
A lazily falling star
That melts in the palm, with millions
More soon floating near and far.

The winter sky's been shaken,
And all its whirling snows
Are strewing the departing year
With petals from a pure white rose.

The encore sends out solar flares,
And then a riverrun,
The dancers dive and tumble –
And "Botanica" is done.

Now back to August – only
A patch in some well-drained loam,
When finally the sun came out,
Promised harvests for the home.

The sun stayed out, however,
And all that insolation
Transformed in less than thirty days
The surviving vegetation.

At Quincy's, sunny faces
All turned to greet the man
Who gave them life and weeded them
And fed them from a can

Of fish emulsion – shades of Squanto –
(And why not have him in this canto?
He must himself have grown such flowers,
As native to his land – now ours).

The dancer, once depressive,
Now flips to his manic pole,
Bill's-Spray-N-Grow-ing every day
With rapture in his soul.

He contemplates a Zebulon,
Whose stars in yellow sprays
Of Fibonacci spirals
Run in dizzy double ways.

A Ring of Fire pulses,
A Grey Stripe like a bird
Sits with its golden feathers
By the breezes gently stirred.

The green cup of a Sunbeam
Is a bowl of buttered peas,
Its swirls of tiny flowerets
Too tight yet for the bees.

Other suns are opening their hearts
Till every ovary conceives,
Their petals drenched in yellow paint,
And pollen dripping on their leaves.

The Cyclops pass out goblets,
Which bees with hairy legs,
Unrolling their proboscises,
Suck down to the last sweet dregs.

Like a bee the dancer closes in
On the bells of the Heavenly Blue,
With creamy throats and saffron
Centers deep in honeydew.

In psychedelic greens the screen
From stem to calyx floods,
With curling sepals looking
Just like sinsemilla buds.

Petals wilt and shrivel,
And seeds begin to gleam,
The camera is an eyeball,
But the image is a dream.

The house and porch fill up with blooms,
The giant plasma screen
In the living room displays each day
A different high-def scene.

One time it's mating grasshoppers
On a bed of flowerets,
Never mind the coming winter,
Theirs is life without regrets.

Now the marigolds, all withered
And black, are otherwise
Just as they were when green and gold,
Before their sad demise.

A lab report confirms that they've
Succumbed to so-called late blight,
And should be burned, which turns
On in the dancer's brain a light.

For one, they're dry as tinder,
Just asking for the match,
The lawn is mown, there's none of that
Old fire-spreading thatch.

And a charitable function's
Been arranged at the house that calls
For Moses to show his marigolds –
The occasion neatly falls.

Besides, we know the dancer,
Like his buddy Bachelard,
Is at heart a common firebug,
Above all in his own backyard:

Those bonfires with the Christmas tree
And sunflowers by the score
At Easter, and for Halloween
See Canto number IV.

The dancers have been summoned
Before the big event
For rehearsal crafted in the form
Of a pyro-experiment,

Involving an inflammable
Liquid or two, to see
How a spectacle can be produced
For the good of society.

And now, the guests have all arrived,
Had drinks, and up they go,
At the sound of a Tibetan bell,
For a view of the field below.

They climb the broad, then narrow stairs,
And pass the tapes in the tower,
And 'ooh' and 'aah' at the spectral sight
Of the dusky solar flower.

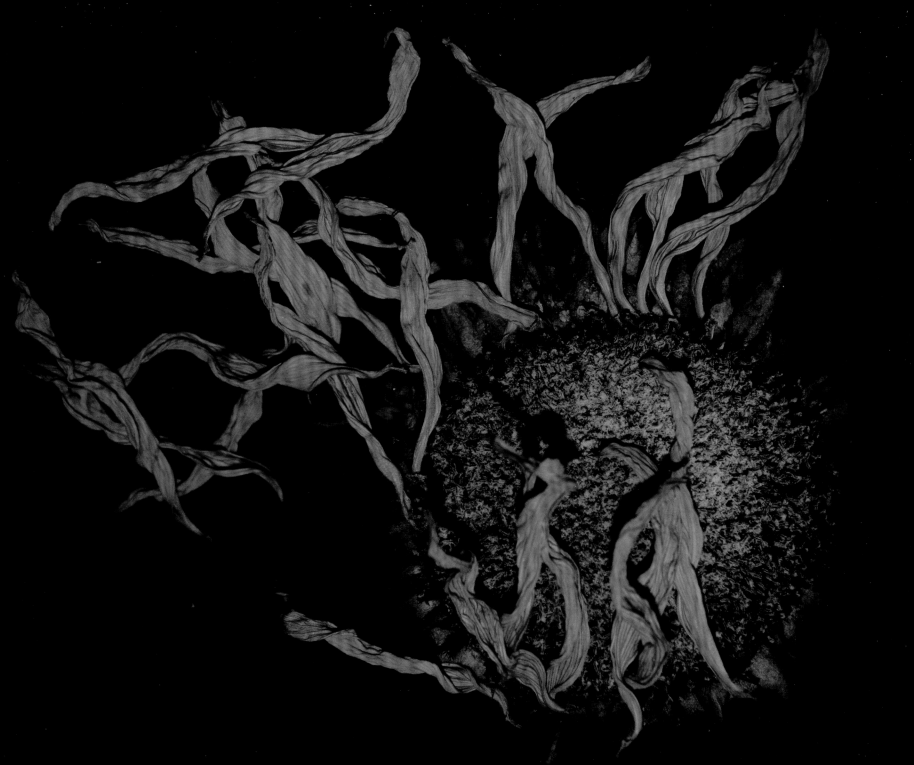

I'm sorry I don't have pictures,
But the charity was clever:
They asked for exclusivity
In all forms whatsoever.

Sixteen almost naked dancers
At the source of every ray,
In the circle sown with clover,
Like living statues stay

Frozen till the signal comes,
And saying private prayers,
They move along the marigolds,
Misting gasoline from sprayers.

A pause – and then it's "Fire!"
And sixteen poised igniters
All squeeze the little triggers
Of their plastic butane lighters,

And sixteen rapid fuses
In a center-seeking whoosh
Find Moses in the middle
Of another burning bush.

He roars, the wildly flaming
Rays surround him where he stands,
At the heart of the sun he's planted
With his own – and some Mexican – hands.

In one converging motion,
The dancers all rush in
To bathe themselves in firelight
And let the fires lick their skin.

The blazes burn two minutes,
The blight is surely toast,
The embers glow and sparkle
At the Mixtecs and the host.

Up at the third floor windows,
The guests are first aghast
That anyone would torch his field
Or it would burn so fast.

"Oh my God!" said some of the women,
"Jesus!" said some of the men,
And a voice called, "Moses, Moses,
Could we please see that again?"

The Fire Marshall never knew,
Though he has known in the past,
The neighbors, used to fires,
Didn't call, and it didn't last.

The troupe and the dancer-arsonist,
With a twinkle in his eye,
Rejoined the party to applause
For a piece of apple pie.

There's nothing like a dose of Momix,
Mixed with wine, to take the edges
Off self-restraint, and in consequence
Many guests increased their pledges.

Then goodbyes, and the season is over,
Before long there's a chill in the air,
The moon is a fading flower,
And the lawn shows its silver hair.

But nature never ceases,
Every force evolves a form,
One seed so far increases
Till each seed head is a swarm.

A twisted Russian Mammoth
Is a chalky human skull,
And other suns so swollen that
They're hemispherical.

Some disks are perfect circles,
With row on spinning row
Of rhombuses apportioned
In the Golden Ratio.

For the dancer, mad for beauty,
Each flower is an icon
Whose light divine he gathers in
Forever with his Nikon.

The memory in his little Mac
Fills often to the core,
Instead of tapes or chips he now
Throws hard drives in the drawer.

Mega – giga – terabytes
Of images and words,
A hundred movies of the wind,
His conversations with the birds.

It's all preserved in silicon,
The amber of the age,
And in more user-friendly form
In the ink on this very page.

An early snowfall whitens
The fields and gives the flowers
Hoods and cloaks like holy men
In an ancient Book of Hours.

A day in complete isolation,
Selecting the few from the plenty,
But no one's surprised when the dancer
Comes out with twelve thousand and twenty.

The fact is he was making more
And still more pictures of the bees,
By playing and overlaying,
And capturing HDVs.

But Cynthia in black in fog
Stalks through the fields like the Reaper,
(The photo's on Ann Leary's blog),
And the dark is getting deeper.

The next two weeks are agony,
But helped by many voices,
And shots of Sugar-Free Red Bull,
The dancer makes his choices.

November comes, and in Milan
A gallery wants a show,
The dancer has twelve thousand shots,
Not to mention his video.

Meanwhile he hasn't been changing
The water in his vases,
And when visitors enter the dining room
There is anguish on their faces.

He wishes he could show them all,
Or merge them into one,
The gallery wants two dozen,
Which is easier said than done.

The flower heads are drying,
But their stalks are slowly rotting
In liquid that's fermenting
With foam until it's clotting.

It's all part of the natural cycle,
Which must end in death and decay –
You and I would have changed that water,
Moses brews it another day.

Then it's poured like a benediction
On forsythia bushes below –
When they blossom profusely in April,
Never doubt what strange milk made them grow.

December: Italy and Spain,
And once again to Greece,
Where Holland is awaiting him,
To fit the final piece

In the puzzle of the dancer's poem,
Never mind it's been twenty-six years
Since he scrawled on some yellow paper
Some verses and asked for veneers.

Moses, is there anything
You'd like to add, or subtract?
And may I use some of your pictures?
"By all means. But you choose. It's my final act."

2009

Epilogue

June

The air was soft and heavy,
And smelled of earth and rain –
The dancer raced the clouds to weed
Again at Quincy Lane.

He takes his Gothic hoe in hand,
Whose blade is like a beak –
Like any other dancer he's
Dependent on technique.

He twirls his hoe, he slices,
He hooks weeds out by the roots,
The grass and vetch go flying,
Untouched the sunflower shoots.

He must be in New York by eight,
He churns like a machine,
Fast-forwarding along the rows,
In a sweat laced with caffeine.

Then suddenly the sky goes dark,
And a single tongue of breeze
Licks up the undersides of leaves,
And whitens all the trees.

The dancer hears approaching
A sound like a speeding train,
Until he's hit full-bodily
By a bursting wall of rain.

The boiling sky's ripped open
By a jagged, flashing blade,
The thunderclap which follows
Explodes like a grenade.

His body sheathed in water,
He buries his steel in the sod,
Its handle tight in his wet hands,
He's a human lightning rod.

He holds his ground, in a fury
He hacks at the weeds in the rows,
He roars at the storm like Lear and Tom,
If he goes in a flash, he goes.

The worst of the front passes over,
The rain becomes gentle, and then,
As he finishes weeding, the sun comes out,
And he gets in his car again.

October

At the house one more producer
Comes to call – Fabrizio –
And the money is in London,
And a plan will make it flow.

But that was back in April,
And the project is on hold,
And now it's almost Halloween,
And the pumpkin's getting cold.

I was there when a man named Gatewood
In a silver limousine
Rolled into what seemed a movie,
With him in the opening scene.

He sat with us and we all discussed
The film we wanted to make,
And each subsequent producer
Has arrived for another take.

The concept was – what was it? –
The man, the house, the dancer,
His way of life, his gardens,
His looking for the answer

In sunlight and in water,
In memory, in romance,
In flower buds, in fire,
And now and again in dance.

We called it "60 Mixtures,"
An invited exposé,
In sixty scenes behind the scenes
To be shot in a year (or a day)

In theaters and on location
In "The Town Where Time Stands Still" –
It was half improvisation
In the beehive of Bell Hill,

In the house like the House of Usher –
It was somewhat in need of repair,
And it rose out of the hilltop like
A castle in the air.

Nothing has changed, fundamentally,
In all of the years since those times,
The dancer's still telling his story,
Like the Mariner – and it still rhymes.

Traveling into the landscape
Of his infinite backyard,
He's gone so far into the garden,
He's come out as the avant-garde,

To a minimum security prison,
Where he's chained to himself alone,
To the grounds of the sanatorium
Where he's found himself a home.

There you will find him sitting
In a dome of leaves or vines –
In these natural confessionals
He'll be waiting to speak his lines,

Where the catbird that mews and whistles
Is still a summer guest,
But with tape teased from a Memorex
No longer lines its nest,

Where the catbird that sings in the bushes
Knows its own lines now by heart,
And will help to prompt the dancer,
Since it's also learned his part.

But wait! A cameraman appears
From Brazil as the harvest comes in,
Since in Rio a month-long Momix run
Of "Botanica"'s soon to begin.

In the studio in the forest,
In the tower, the garden, the hall,
The visitor asks if he's dreaming,
As the wallpaper drops from the wall.

Then he's off with some curious footage,
Which a million Brazilians will see,
And marvel what tribe and what shaman
Create dance in the land of the free.

The dancer, well shot, retires to his Adirondack chair
In the circle that's raked like a stage,
He lights a match, smoke rises
And curls into the crystal autumn air
In the shape of a poem on a page.

2010

photo credits

All photographs by
Moses Pendleton, except:

Phil Holland:
pp. 12, 13. 25, 32, 43, 65, 66

Max Pucciarello:
pp. 46, 52 (top), 72, 73, 74, 75

John Dreyfus/M. Pendleton: p. 18

Eddy Fernandez: p. 95

Photographer unknown: p. 30

DESIGN:
Leslie Noyes Creative Consulting